BET ON YOURSELF

5 Approaches To Winning

CoWano Stanley

Copyright © 2020 By CoWano Stanley

All rights reserved. No part of this publication may be reproduced, distributed, or transmitted in any form or by any means including photocopying, recording, or other electronic or mechanical methods, without the prior written permission of the publisher, except in the case of brief quotations embodied in critical reviews and specific other noncommercial uses permitted by copyright laws.

Title: Bet on Yourself

Subtitle: 5 Approaches to Winning

Author: CoWano Stanley

ISBN 978-0-578-64831-6

Publisher: CoWano Publishing, Inc.

Cover Design: Ismail Ben Design Group

Web: www.ismailben.com

Facebook: Ismail Ben

Instagram: ismail_ben_design_group

Follow Ms. CoWano "Coco" Stanley on Social Media

 cowanococostanley   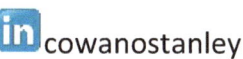 cowanostanley

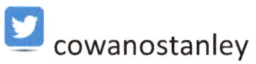 cowanostanley    lovme_coco

cowanostanley.com

"You don't become what you want, you become what you believe."

~Oprah Winfrey~

"It doesn't matter if a million people tell you what you can't do, or if 10 million tell you no. If you get one yes from God, that's all you need."

~Tyler Perry~

Table of Contents

Acknowledgment……………………………………………7

Introduction…………………………………………………9

Chapter 1: Winning……………………………………11

- Mindset of Winning

Chapter 2: Taking a Leap of Faith……………17

- Believing in Your Potential
- Habits

Chapter 3: Taking a Risk……………………………31

- Investing (Mind, Body, Soul)

Chapter 4: The 3 P………………………………………41

- Patience
- Persistence
- Perseverance

Chapter 5: Staying Focus……………………………49

Reflect, Act, Win: Self-Help Questions………53

About the Author…………………………………………57

Other Books to Purchase……………………………59

Acknowledgment

First, I would like to give God all the praise, glory, and honor for me writing this book. He has blessed me in many ways, time after time. I never knew that I would ever write one book. However, this is my second self-published book, and I have been blessed to be a co-author in 2 collaboration books. So, to God, I am very humble and grateful for all he has done. Through all the ups and downs, I have gone through on this journey called life; I thank him for getting me through it. Going through some of the hardest times of my life, I would not have made it this far without God. I will forever be faithful and grateful to God.

Writing this book has taught me that I don't need validation from anyone but God. I know that I will be great and successful in whatever I do. It has also taught me that no matter how small or big my situation is, I must trust God in them all. Holding on to faith and trust in God will help me every time. He is the one that, in his due time, the right doors will open, and the wrong doors will close. You must praise God through the open doors and the closed doors.

I also would like to give thanks to my mother Nancy and Aunt Gloria, who always give me great words of encouragement with everything in life. They always provide me with nothing but the best of love and support no matter what. I love you both.

To my other half Michael of 11 years. With all the ups and downs, good and bad times. You have been there to help to learn how not to panic. So, when times get a little rough, I need to stop and come up with a solution. Shutting down and giving up should not be an option but to keep going and make things happen. You give me the good hard criticism that I sometimes need, although it doesn't feel right, it is well required. Thank you very much. I love you.

Lastly, I would like to thank some great people that I can genuinely call friends that have been there for me when I was writing this book as well as the support that they have given me over time; Frances, Lydashia, Patricia, and Jaini. These ladies were always there when I text or called during the process of this book. Thank you, ladies, for putting up with me. I love you.

Introduction

What does it mean to bet on yourself? Hummmm! When I think about betting on yourself, I think of the idea of going into a casino and taking your money to win and hit big. Of course, everyone that goes into a casino wants to win and hit big. Well, when it comes to betting on yourself in life, I think about taking a chance on deciding, taking a risk and having faith to accomplish goals and dreams that your heart desires to do. This can be in areas of your career, business, health, finances, spiritually, or even mentally. But to do that, you must get rid of the fears, doubts, and excuses that keep you bound from moving forward. You can't take a chance on yourself if you allow those things to stop you.

Going to new levels, a new position, and unknown territory in your life can be quite scary. Believe me, I know. There are many things I have an approach that I was afraid to try or move forward with because I thought of all the what if it didn't go right, and what if I failed, etc. But because I wanted to win in those areas, I had to step out there and put my foot forward. However, the biggest thing I had to do was, trust God through the journey and listen to God for direction.

With men this is impossible, but with God, all things are possible

(Matthews 19:26)

If you are reading this book right now and you know you are not betting on yourself so that you can win, you need to go ahead and decide to move forward and step out, take a chance on you and win.

If you want different results, you must do something different or take a different approach

~Albert Einstein~

Getting started on whatever your heart desires is one of the steps needed. As you read this book, I hope it helps you to go ahead and start taking the action necessary for you to win in life.

The best thing I ever did was believe in me

~Unknown~

Chapter 1: Winning

Let's begin with what is winning. This is one approach that is needed to win in life. Everyone's idea of winning is not the same. Some people think winning is when they are financially stable. Yes, that is winning. Some people think winning is setting a particular goal to pay off debt. Yes, that is winning also. If you set a goal to lose a certain amount of weight by a deadline, and you reach that goal. Then yes, that is winning also. Winning is more than just the examples I gave. The definition of winning is gaining something or winning in something you have set out to achieve. If you set a goal to accomplish something and you complete that goal, then you win. Too many times, I hear people put others down because they are not winning, the way they think or feel you should be winning or what they consider is a win. Everyone's definition of winning can be different. What you set out for yourself to accomplish is your way of winning. So, no one tells you what your win is.

Winning means you're willing to go longer, work harder, and give more than anyone else

~Vince Lombardi~

Remember this:

PROPER PLANNING AND PRACTICE PREVENT PISS POOR PERFORMANCE

Mindset of Winning

Now that we have determined what winning means let's talk about the mindset of winning. You must choose to wake up and win if you want to win. Your day will be determined based on your attitude. Keeping that positive attitude every day will help you towards that goal of winning. And of course, you can't win without God either. When you have a thought or an idea of something you want to accomplish, it is a must that you have a winning mindset & attitude. Your attitude will determine your altitude. If your vision is to win, no matter what that may be, your action and mindset will show that as you keep pushing to the result of winning. Your mindset will determine how far you will go. Do you have a mindset of winning in life?

Winning takes precedence overall. There's no gray area. No Almost.

~Kobe Bryant~

Now keeping a positive winning mindset is not going to be easy because life has a way of bringing people and things down your path to discourage you from that winning mindset. 80% of our thoughts are psychological. So, in that case, that means we should have control over our thoughts and not allow everything to come in, and it controls us. Yes, unfortunate circumstances & situations do come into our life & may disrupt our mindset. But what we don't have to do is stay there and live in it. If you want to win in life and keep that winning mindset, you have the power to control what you allow to come in.

The secret of success is learning how to use pain and pleasure instead of having pain and pleasure using you. If you do that, you're in control of your life; if you don't, life controls you.

~Tony Robbins~

So, if you set your mind to tell yourself that no matter the circumstances or situations I may face, I am going to win. So, you believe in it and act; then, you will win. Winning isn't just an action; it is required that you keep your mind in check to stay positive while believing that you are going to win. It is easy for discouragement, fear, doubt, depression, etc. to show up at your doorstep when reality shows you something different from your belief and vision. But it's up to you to close the door on these negative or bad things that knock at your door.

If you stay positive in a negative situation, then you win.

~Unknown~

At the end of the day, winning is up to you. No one is going to push you as you will. If you want something bad enough, you will make things happen.

Some people watch things happen, some people make things happen, and some don't know what happens to stay out of the last category 3.

~Stormy Wellington~

Winners focus on winning; losers focus on winners

~Eric Thomas~

Chapter 2: Taking a Leap of Faith

Taking a leap of faith is another approach that is necessary if you want to win. It's not always easy to jump out there and take a leap into what you want. Now it does cross most of our minds when stepping out into the unknown. The what-ifs and thought of failing come up.

You can't be afraid to fail; it's the only way you succeed.

~Lebron James~

When wanting to accomplish some goals and dreams, you do know that it's not going to just fall in your lap. Yes, God will help along the way, but you must take action to take the first step in the process. The first step in doing that is getting started. Talking to people will do nothing until you start. Some people will tell you that you can't do it, or you're not a winner, that's too hard for you to do and so on. But you must follow your heart and God to direct you.

Trust in the Lord with all your heart; do not depend on your own understanding. Seek his will in all you do, and he will show you which path to take. (Proverbs 3:5-6 NLT)

The good thing is when you do get started and take that leap of faith, you do more than the people who never started at all. Don't let what other people don't do or never do stop you from climbing higher. The sky is limited, and so is success.

Fear may rise up, but faith always wins

~Unknown~

One day I was watching and listening to a YouTube video where the actor, businessman, entertainer, producer, comedian, and philanthropist Steve Harvey was talking about jumping. The point he was making was that if you never jump, you will never know that you can fly. When you first jump out there, it is not going to be easy. There will be some rough patches you will hit; you will get some bruises and failures on the journey of that jump. But don't you give up. If you keep going, keep pushing, keep moving & keep trying, on the path to winning the way will get a little smoother. Even when that path gets smoother every now and then, you may hit a rough spot again, but this is a part of the process called life. Also, everyone is not going to agree or understand the decision you are making. The vision that God gives you is for you to see. So, stop trying to get or force everyone to see or agree with the view that is provided to you. When you are taking a leap of faith, it's just that FAITH.

> Faith is the substance of things hoped for, and the evidence of things not seen (Hebrews 11:1 KJV)

You must know in your heart and mind that faith is going to get you to that destination you are trying to reach. By taking the leap of faith, God will carry you through it all. But it's up to you to take that leap of faith. No one is going to make it for you – not to mention no one can take the jump for you. If you want to Win, you can, but it starts when you take the leap of faith.

Now take a moment to write some things that are holding you back from taking a leap of faith.

1._____

2._____

3._____

4._____

5._____

Believing in Your Potential

In life, you must learn what your potential is. Let's look at what is potential. Potential is having or showing the capacity to become or develop into something in the future. So, with potential, you can change what's in you to become something better. The potential in you to do something better in life, you must realize and believe in your potential. Everyone has the potential to be higher. You can find safety and peace in realizing your potential then taking your potential and developing, growing, and maturing that into something more significant. It's so easy for others to see the potential in you and believe what you can become. However, it will just stay a potential and nothing more because that individual is not taking the action that's needed. To win, you must believe in your potential. If you just believe in your potential to do something more than where you are with it, it can open doors you never even imagined would open. It will take work within yourself to mature, grow, and develop in all areas of our life to win. Take a chance on what God has put in you and win. There is more work that needs to be done in all of us. And the only way to become better is by first believing in yourself that you can do better and be better.

Do you know what potential you have that can be developed?

1._____

2._____

3._____

4._____

5._____

What are some things you can do to start to develop them?

_____

_____

_____

_____

Believe in your potential

~Unknow~

Habits

Habits are things that most of us will have a hard time changing. This is an approach needed to win. Habits can be an advantage and a disadvantage in our life. Did you know that some of our habits are due to the fact we have not learned anything new? Some of those old habits you keep making & repeating are a hindrance in your life. To win, you must learn how to discipline yourself and get rid of the bad/old habits that are not helping you to win. You must develop a new pattern that is good and helpful for you to win now. It's time for you to adjust, download, and update new habits that are beneficial in that area of your life that you want to win in. Some habits that we have had may have been suitable only for that season in our life. However, those same habits may not be right for where you want to go next in your experience of a new season and journey. Each season will require new and different habits and equipment. So, you must adjust and change those to fit for the new you, new mindset, and new level.

We cannot solve problems with the same thinking we used when we created them

~Albert Einstein~

Which habits are holding you back or keeping you from moving forward? Take a moment and write out your habits that are an advantage and disadvantage in your life.

Advantages:

1._____

What can I do to develop/change this habit or do nothing to this habit?

_____

2._____

What can I do to develop/change this habit or nothing to this habit?

_____

3._____

What can I do to develop/change this habit or nothing to this habit?

_____

4._____

What can I do to develop/change this habit or nothing to this habit?

_____

5. _____

What can I do to develop/change this habit or nothing to this habit?

_____

Disadvantages:

1._____

What can I do to change this habit or get rid of it?

_____

2._____

What can I do to change this habit or get rid of it?

_____

3._____

What can I do to change this habit or get rid of it?
_____

4._____

What can I do to change this habit or get rid of it?

_____

5._____

What can I do to change this habit or get rid of it?

_____

Now that you have written down your habits, whether they are good or bad, you can start to see where changes can be made or developed. If you want to win in your personal, business, career, or whatever area in your life, changing some of those habits that are not helping you will help you to see the change you want to see. Take a chance on you to win; habits are one of the most challenging things to change. Some of the habits we all have are so comfortable that we would somewhat not change them. Trying something new and different feels weird and uncomfortable. But if you speak to some of the most successful and wealthiest people in the world, they will more than likely tell you that being comfortable did not get them to where they are. But being in an unknown and uncomfortable position leads them to open opportunities.

The comfort zone will never get you to higher levels. So, start working, praying, and asking God to help you change some of the habits you have listed. It is often stated that if you do something consistently for 21 days, it will become a habit. Making these changes in habits that are hindering your growth, you will begin to see different results that you want to win in. Take a chance on you and win by making adjudgments and getting rid of some of the habits you have listed.

Great things never come from comfort zones

~Unknown~

Chapter 3: Taking a Risk

Many people do not like taking risks. A risk is an approach that the majority would rather play it safely. Especially when it comes to things like our money and health. Let's look at what risk means; the risk is a possibility or chance of loss. Risk is usually a 50 to 50 chance something will or will not work out. But if you don't take a risk at all, you have chosen not even to try to see if you will receive the other 50% to win. I get it; not everyone is a risk taker even when it comes to betting on yourself and your future. Have you ever thought that we take a risk every day as we go on with life each day? You have no clue on how the day is going to go, good or bad. You may even plan your day, but it doesn't mean things will go the way you expect it (again good or bad).

Yes, taking a risk with some goals, investments, careers, etc., can be a hard decision to make. Decision making is a part of life. Risk can be a loss or a gain. Risk has uncertainty attached to it. The possibility can sometimes be more of an impossible situation against you than for you. But don't let the word FEAR stop you from taking a risk. A hopeless situation can turn into a huge possibility. One thing that you can do is write out the pros and cons of every chance you are thinking about taking. Whether that risk is leaving a job, starting your own business full time, moving to a new city or state, changing careers, or relationship change in your personal life or business. Whatever it is, weigh out the options. But doing nothing is not the answer unless God has specifically

spoken to your heart to be still just for a moment. Sometimes it is not the season for us to make certain moves/risks. Only you, on your journey, will know when the time is.

Let's take me as an example. I left my job in accounting for four years at a company to start my own cleaning business. It was not an easy decision, but in my spirit, it was right. Not many in my circle agreed it was the right decision. However, had I not taken that jump, that risk, etc. I would not have experienced some hardships of learning what it means to run a business. I would not have experienced being on my schedule. There were events I would not have been able to attend. And the discipline of getting up to work my schedule no matter because I don't get a dependent work check and so on. So, I took the risk, but I do not regret it because it has helped me evolve and learn a lot in my time. I had to take the chance even if no one understood my process or steps to take the leap. Being able to receive something sometimes is essential. And for me, if I didn't leave the 7- 5 job, I would not have been able to do certain things because my time would have required me to be at the job anywhere from 9 – 13 hours a day doing the accounting on their clock, not mines.

    Take a chance on yourself and your future so that new doors and opportunities can be opened. But if you want to win, take a chance on you. Don't sit back and let your fears take control over what can become or opportunity doors opening because you decide not to take the risk.

Investing (Mind, Body, & Soul)

There are many ways to invest in yourself. Investing sometimes consists of time, not just money. Then there are things like going to a conference, seminar, buying training courses, getting a coach, or even putting money into something for a return profit. I look at investing in all these areas as a way of sowing a seed. At some point, these investments can give you a positive outcome. You may not see the result right away, but the result will come. Invest in yourself to become a better you are necessary because we can all be better in some way.

Are you investing in yourself? What are things doing to invest in your mind, body and soul?

1._____

2._____

3._____

4._____

5._____

One thing I believe is a must that we invest in daily is our mind. Mediating on God for me is the first that I do, allowing God to help me reflect on myself and looking at myself in the mirror to see what things I must change to see a clear vision. Also, reading different books, listening to audios, and feeding it with new and different positive information.

Your mind is so powerful, and if you feed it with the right information and knowledge, it will put you in the proper position and places that you desire to get to or at. Also, feeding your mind with positive information will help you mentally. I am no way a professional psychiatrist, but I do know that it is easy to go into depression, frustration, or overwhelming with life when your mind is on a breaking point. If your mind is not in a functional space, it also affects your spirit (soul), your energy. Energy is everything. If you have no power to be positive, uplifting, motivated, etc. then you won't have the mind to win. I believe that sometimes God can't bless us with specific blessings (that are for you) because our way of thinking has not changed. He doesn't want us to have a blessing prematurely. So, the mind is always a great thing to invest in. It is also good to invest in our physical health. Yes, this investment could be expensive, but it is worth it. If your health isn't right, then you are not good. Your body needs rest as well. Get adequate rest when needed. So, take care of yourself as much as you can.

    So, if you want to win, you must invest in getting what you want to see a result. Yes, I do invest in myself. I have spent a lot of money on learning a lot of knowledge in certain areas. The latest thing I have invested in is; learning how to do Wholesale real estate & became a member of Urban CEO. We live in a world where coaches or highly paid successful people don't have time to go everywhere to teach. So, their teaching is recorded into a course, and the course is sold online to the world to purchase. I also buy lots of books to read, which I love to do. Some of the inspiring and motivational books I read are:

- The Bible- different version
- Think and Grow Rich by Napoleon Hill
- 9 Laws of Success by Stormy Wellington
- Secrets of a Millionaire Mind by T. Harv Eker
- Rich Dad Poor Dad by T. Kiyosaki
- The Four Agreements by Don Miguel Ruiz
- Destiny by T.D. Jakes
- A Six-Figure Vision by Taurea "Vision" Avant
- How not to be a Broke Author by Taurea "Vision" Avant

When I do personal meditation time, I read then I listen to audios of some successful people I follow such as:

- Tony Robbins
- Stormy Wellington
- Les Brown
- Eric Thomas
- Lisa Nichols
- Steve Harvey
- T.D. Jakes

So, as you see, I take my mind very seriously when it comes to investing in it, to keep an excellent sanity mindset. So, find out what works for you that will help you to win with your mind, body, and soul.

Price is what you pay. Value is what you get

~Warren Buffett~

We don't have to be smarter than the rest We have to be more disciplined than the rest

~Warren Buffett~

Chapter 4: The 3 P's

The three things that I will talk about in this chapter are patience, persistence, and perseverance. All three of these approaches are very critical to have as well as one of the hardest things to do. Due to the fact all three consist of time. So, let's jump right into these three now.

Patience

Let's start with what patience is. Patience is willing to wait or remain calm until something happens. We all have or still have a hard time being patient. With the way the world and people operate now, everything is quick and fast, and no one wants to wait for anything. Everyone is in a rush to make things happen or to get somewhere. But in certain situations, it's not meant to be quick. Great things come with process and time. For example, when it comes to wanting to have a successful business, know that it is not going to happen overnight. Wanting a company to be successful is a process. Another example is that any kind of relationship (personal or business) does not become successful overnight. It comes with patience and time. Some things must take place before getting fruitful results. Even if you want to win and be successful as an individual in life, there are steps you cannot skip. You will not get the same results from completing all the steps vs. skipping steps.

There are no elevators to success you have to take the stairs

~Unknown~

If you do want to win in your career, business, relationships, health, or whatever it is, patience is one that you must learn to have in the process.

Patience is not passive waiting. Patience is active acceptance of the process required to attain your goals and dreams.

~Ray A. Davis~

Write down some things that you can be more patient with.

1._____

2._____

3._____

4._____

5._____

Persistence

Now, this word persistence is a word that many of you probably have a hard time sticking to it. If you want to win in areas of your life, you will need to be persistent. Persistence is the ability to stick with something. Now, how many times have you started something and didn't stick to it nor finish it? Some people will switch like the wind blows, never doing anything long enough to see if it will work.

A river cuts through a rock not because of its power, but its persistence.

~Unknown~

Now the things you wrote for Patience are you being persistent with those & if not why?

_____
_____
_____
_____

After writing your answer up above, do you see where you can make some changes in areas that you are not persistent in? I am pretty sure we all, at one time or another, started something and didn't see the results we wanted right away, so we stopped. We didn't see it until the end. If you stop, right now, and think about some of the things that you did not stay persistent with, most of you would say you didn't have time, didn't see the results I wanted, lost focus, and so on. When you start something, you must have the drive to continue with it and not get sidetracked or bored with it. It is always a fast-exciting rush for most of us that starts something at the beginning of what we call a great idea or opportunity. But along the way, you begin not to be so excited about it anymore.

An excellent example is when people start in a Network marketing company, a new job, or even start college. The excitement is there at the beginning. However, as weeks and months go by, your attitude of persistence has left you. You no longer want to continue it. Look at the end of the day you are responsible for your motivation and drive to keep going no matter what. You must remind yourself why you started.

Before you start something, write down what is your biggest WHY you are doing it. Keep that as a refresher to keep being persistent and pushing towards the goal. You can do it, so believe it and stay consistent and persistent.

There is no magic to achievement. It's really about hard work, choices, and persistence.

Michelle Obama

Perseverance

With a word like perseverance, like me, I will keep going despite the challenge. The word perseverance means to continue to push through doing something despite the difficulty or how long it will take to achieve the goal. Do you persevere through some things that you have set out to do? When you want to win in an area of your life, you will continue to persevere until you reach that goal. Nothing will make you give up on it.

So, let's not get tired of doing what is good. At just the right time we will reap a harvest of blessings if we don't give up (Galatians 6:9 NLT)

Everything has a time when it is due to be accomplished. It is not only God's timing, but it is also up to you to keep persevering until the goal is met. Winning in life is not about how fast you can get there. Just pace yourself on the journey.

Great things come from hard work and perseverance. No Excuses."

~Kobe Bryant~

"I have observed something else under the sun. The fastest runner doesn't always win the race, and the strongest warrior doesn't always win the battle. The wise sometimes go hungry, and the skillful are not necessarily wealthy. And those who are educated don't always lead successful lives. It is all decided by chance, by being in the right place at the right time

(Ecclesiastes 9:11 NLT)

So, continue the race and push through the challenges that will come along with the journey of reaching the goals and dreams you have set for yourself or your family. The only person that can stop you from persevering is yourself. Nothing is impossible.

It always seems impossible until it's done

~Nelson Mandela~

Fall in love with the process and the results will come.

~Eric Thomas~

Chapter 5: Staying focus

Focus is an approach that must be taken to win. Where you put your attention is where your energy goes. So, if you want to win in a specific area of your life, then put your focus and thinking. We all had several times in our life, where we allowed things or people to get us sidetracked and off focus from our goal. When you want to win in a specific area of your life, you must discipline yourself to stay focused. It's funny how sometimes you set a goal to do something, and as soon as you start it, things and people out of nowhere begin trying to take up your focus time for that goal. You get calls to go here or there or to do something that is not tied to or beneficial for your set goal. But at that moment, that's when you must keep yourself on track and say thanks, but no thanks. Okay, let's be clear; it is okay to say NO to people or things. There is a saying that says, "Work now and play later." Achieve your goals first, then play later. You must stop explaining to people why you can't do something or go somewhere. If you are focused on trying to get something done, then make sure you are setting the necessary time for putting it towards your goal. If it's not about your goal, then let it go. If you want to win, you must do what's needed to stay focused.

Are you focused on your target goal? I know sometimes circumstances and situations can get us in a place that has us off the focus of our goal. And when we get off focus, it takes that much longer to achieve the goal and to get back on fire about the purpose we wanted. The moment you notice you are off-tasked and not focused on something you want to achieve and see those winning results; you need to check yourself and get back on track.

What things are keeping you from focusing on winning?

1._____

2._____

3._____

4._____

5._____

One of the things you can do to stay focused is to set deadlines for those goals. Setting deadlines can help you stay focused on the target. This will help you to know how to set your time daily to work on the goal that you want to achieve. Have you set deadlines for your goals? Now, as you stay focused to win, try to stay consistent, and watch results come to pass.

In the end, we all want a win in our life. But to win, it takes work and time. Most do not want to do what it will take to win. That's why the 1-3% percent is wealthy, and the other 97-99 % is struggling. Changing your mindset, ways, behavior, speaking, etc. is what it will take to start winning in the areas that you desire. Look if it was easy, everyone would be doing it. There is not quick or fast around winning. There is no need for you to rush to get to the finish line. Stay on the course of your journey enjoy every moment and celebrate your accomplishments along the way. The ball is in your court and in your hands to determine if you want to win. No one can win for you. So, go through the process, time, and work, and you will see yourself with the WINS.

"Reflect, Act, Win: Self-Help Questions for Betting on Yourself"

What does 'betting on yourself' mean to you, and how can you start embracing this mindset in your daily life?

_____
_____
_____
_____

What personal strengths can you leverage to create opportunities for winning in your career or personal life?

_____
_____
_____
_____

What limiting beliefs are holding you back from fully betting on yourself, and how can you start reframing them?

_____
_____

_____

_____

When faced with a difficult decision, how can you remind yourself to trust your instincts and make choices that reflect confidence in your abilities?

_____

_____

_____

_____

How do you define 'winning' in your life, and what steps can you take to make it more attainable by betting on yourself?

_____

_____

_____

_____

What are some past decisions where you doubted yourself, and how would the outcome have changed if you had fully trusted your abilities?

_____

_____

_____

_____

How can you develop a support system or network that encourages you to bet on yourself and take bold actions?

_____

_____

_____

_____

What specific goals can you set that align with the principles of betting on yourself, and what actions can you take today to move towards them?

_____

_____

_____

_____

What strategies can you adopt to manage fear and self-doubt when you take risks in pursuit of your goals?

_____
_____
_____
_____

How can you turn failures or setbacks into learning experiences that reinforce the importance of betting on yourself?

_____
_____
_____
_____

About the Author

CoWano Stanley is a speaker, author, and confidence coach who focuses on empowering women to reclaim and increase their confidence, especially those who have experienced trauma or challenging life situations. She was born in Arkansas but grew up in Minneapolis, MN. She resides in Las Vegas, Nevada, and has a diverse background that includes earning two Master's degrees in Business Administration and Accounting and Financial Management and is currently in a Doctoral program. CoWano's journey into confidence coaching stems from her personal experiences of overcoming significant challenges as a single parent and surviving abusive relationships. Her struggles with confidence have fueled her passion for helping other women regain their self-assurance and pursue their goals with vigor. She is a self-published 5X author, including her newest book "The Power of Confidence - 7 Ways to Reclaim & Ignite Your Confidence,". She has collaborated on 9 book projects, 3 being with figures such as Les Brown and Dr. Cheryl Wood. CoWano has been featured in various media outlets and has delivered keynotes and workshops at numerous conferences. She is the visionary behind "The Reclaim Your Confidence Annual Conference in Las Vegas, NV. She is dedicated to helping women increase their confidence to unlock their full potential so they can achieve their goals.

As a business owner, CoWano knows it takes hard work, dedication, and motivation to make things happen. CoWano's mission in life is to help inspire and encourage others so that they can accomplish any goal or dream they desire and bet on themselves. She has more goals she wants to achieve still, but it all takes time and patience as well as a process to get to the finish line. No matter how long it takes or the obstacles that you must go through to get there to never give up, and always believe in yourself. You will have some Wins, and you will have some losses along the way but keep pushing and moving forward, as there is always a light at the end of the tunnel. But most importantly, always keep God first, and he will direct your path along the way.

Other Books by CoWano Stanley

Purchase through her website:

www.cowanostanley.com/books

Self-Published:
- The Power of Confidence: 7 Ways to Reclaim & Ignite Your Confidence
- The Confidence Effect: 45 Strategies to Become a Bold & Confident Go-Getter
- Bet On Yourself: 5 Approaches to Winning
- It's Time to Live
- The Drive of an Entrepreneur: 7 Traits You Must Acquire

Anthology Books (Co-Author)
- Life of Entrepreneur
- From Employee to Entrepreneur
- Mind over Matter
- You Are Enough
- Unleash Your Undeniable Impact
- All Gas No Breaks
- Dare to Rise Above Mediocrity
- Push Through to Breakthrough
- Girl Boss Up

Notes Taking

Notes Taking

www.ingramcontent.com/pod-product-compliance
Lightning Source LLC
Chambersburg PA
CBHW041757040426
42446CB00005B/233